Your Journey to
Personal Power ..... for life
Workbook

Your Journey

Knowledge
is
Power

always REMEMBER
YOU ARE BRAVER
THAN YOU BELIEVE
STRONGER
THAN YOU SEEM
SMARTER
THAN YOU THINK
AND LOVED
-MORE THAN YOU KNOW-

LIFE

~ is a ~

JOURNEY

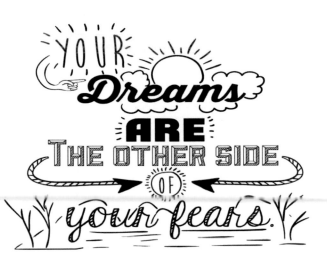

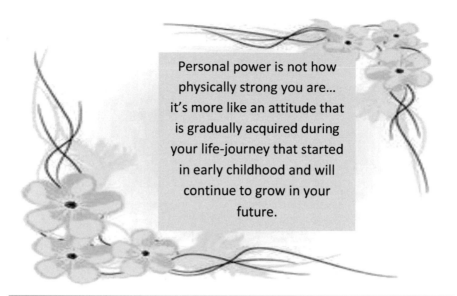

Personal power is not how physically strong you are... it's more like an attitude that is gradually acquired during your life-journey that started in early childhood and will continue to grow in your future.

Positive personal power is based on vision and positive personal qualities. The outer 'you' can be described as how others see you... your appearance and the things you do, but positive empowerment comes from how you see yourself....your inner 'you' characteristics.

Positive empowerment is a merging of self-esteem and self-confidence with the belief that you have the personal skills and resources to affect your life circumstances.

Examples of positive actions that show positive personal power include:

- Being assertive so that your ideas are heard and you may respectfully challenge the ideas of others.
- Expressing ideas and reasons to convince someone of your point of view.
- Making compromises and concessions to reach outcomes that align with your integrity.
- Building respectful relationships.

Negative personal power is the use of manipulation, coercion, or force to control others.

We become what we think about ourselves and how we think of ourselves is the kind of life we live.

When we're trying to overcome a negative self-image and replace it with self-confidence, it's important to make adjustments to our negative thinking and beliefs about ourselves.

This journey of self-exploration will guide you to make those adjustments which will improve your confidence, self-esteem and personal power.

Let your journey to personal power for life — begin !!

This Is SOOO Me...

My Name
&
Nickname

I live
With

Favorite
Subject &
Teacher

Favorite
Music

3 Words That Describe Me

I Was Born To...

I Treasure...

3 Words That Describe My
Friends

I love....

I am usually:
early _ _
or late_ _

I am more of a
cat _ _   or
dog _ _
person

I stand for...

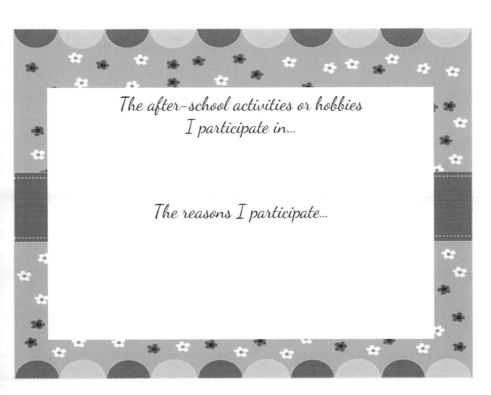

The after-school activities or hobbies
I participate in...

The reasons I participate...

Would you rather...

...be without internet for a week, or without your phone?

... make a phone call or send a text?

...put a stop to war or end world hunger?

...be able to fly or be invisible?

eat chocolate covered
5 crickets or 25 ants?

...always have the same song stuck in your head or always have the same dream at night?

...write a book and have it made into a movie or star in the movie of your favorite book?

What I wish other
people would get about
me...

With all my heart

I wish.....

Self-Esteem

The more you like yourself, accept yourself and respect yourself....
the higher your self-esteem is.

Those who base self-esteem on positive inner qualities are more likely to have healthier self-esteem than those who base it on negative factors such as what they look like or if they are a part of a certain group.

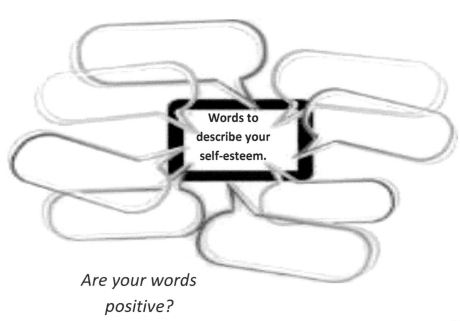

Words to describe your self-esteem.

Are your words positive?

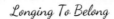

Longing To Belong

Belonging to a group of friends provides connections and that can be wonderful but it can also have problems such as the pressure to look or act in certain ways in order to maintain the connection.

Sometimes girls are willing to do things that go against their beliefs or values... or they may do things that they really don't want to do in order to maintain their connection to the group.

Why is it hard for some to say no to their friends?

How might someone with strong personal power react to friends who ask them to do things that go against their beliefs or values?

What are some things you would just not do?

Describe Your Absolute # 1 BFF

Describe your relationship in detail. What do you do... what do you talk about... or laugh about... or cry about?
What do you do when your friend is upset?

Describe your group of BFFs in detail.

When do you hang out... what do you do...
what do you talk about? Laugh about?
Where do you go?

What Are Your Thoughts About the Following Characteristics

Trustworthy · Respectful · Caring · Honest · Tolerant · Empathetic · Helpful · Pride in Self & Others · Cooperative · Compassionate · Understanding · Fair · Stand Up for Self

How would you describe a person or a cool sister-hood group with those characteristics? What would they do? Where might you find them? What might they sound like?

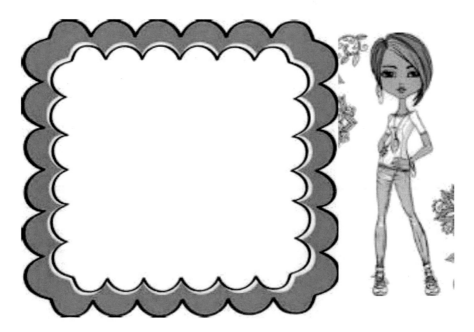

How would friends in a really cool 'sister-hood' group with those characteristics treat you? How would they make you feel?

Do you feel that you are a part of a really cool 'sister–hood' type group? If you are not... would you want to be? And why?

Is someone you know a part of a group that may not have that cool 'sister-hood' feel?

Do you believe those group members basically trust, support and have respect for each other and for others?

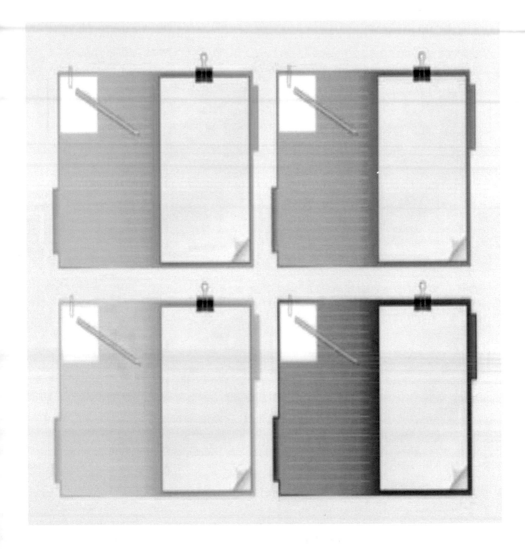

Girls Who Act Mean

Do you know of any girls who hurt others on purpose? Maybe some have even formed a clique? Some say hurtful things about someone... maybe about their weight, or their clothing.

Some act as though they are better than others • Some Gossip • Look down upon others • Exclude • Spread lies and rumors

What are other ways they hurt others?

Describe any mean experiences that have happened to you or to someone else.

How did it make you feel to experience it or to witness it?

Do you believe that a *mean* girl shows
that she understands what her victim is going
through? Or helps her to feel that she's
not alone?

Describe your feelings about whether you believe a
sister-hood girl shows that she understands
what others are going through and helps them to
feel that they're not alone and that she cares?

Girls Who Malign Other Girls Destroy Themselves

Of course everyone has disagreements with others and working that out is ok... but Hayley Morgan writes in her book 'the dateable rules'... that girls shouldn't fight other girls....ever.

She goes on to say that when girls fight other girls they are not only hurting themselves, they are also hurting all girls who come after them.

She suggests that girls should be encouraging each other to reach for the stars instead of plotting against each other.

What could she mean... they are not only hurting themselves, they are also hurting all girls who come after them?

Empower Yourself

In case you or someone you know becomes a target of a girl who harasses others, your best bet is to plan how you will respond to her efforts to make you upset.

Bullying is about power and she wants you to believe you're a nothing.

Assertive responses show that you believe in yourself. Just keep believing in yourself and know that you have the power.

Some assertive girls practice until they become comfortable in calmly standing up for themselves (and others) to bullying, cyberbullying, sexual bullying and sexting.

They also know when they need adult intervention.

Assertive Responses

Don't let her know that your feelings are hurt
- Don't run away crying
- Act like you truly don't care
- Be nice to her
- Respond with kindness
- Smile like you mean it.

When they are whispering while you're nearby, pretend you don't hear a thing.

Cyber Intimidators enjoy the reactions of fear and anger, so do not respond or reply to harassing emails, voice mails, text messages, instant messages or blog posts and don't respond to upsetting photographs.

Don't reply to anything that is abusive or obscene.
You or your parents can contact your server to report it.

Defend others if you see it happening. You may have to wait until a little later and ask her if she is okay. You never know if this could be the person that helps you get through your problem.

Go on YouTube and listen to these songs: Mean Girls by Rachel Crow, Mean by Taylor Swift

Another assertive way to respond to those who bully is to use your body language to send a message.

You can practice at home by acting out your responses.

Practice:
- **ways to show you are ignoring.**
- **saying 'so' and using your body to show that s/he isn't bothering you.**
- **confidently walking away.**
- **pretending not to care.**

Remember: for dangerous bullying situations that cause fear, it probably isn't safe to respond. It's important to talk to an adult about the situation.

Are there other safe ways to respond?

Self-Talk

The illustration on the next page represents you.

Silently tell her all of the negative things you believe about yourself...

or the negative things that others have said about you.

Maybe you have become to believe some of the negative words.

Self-Talk

To illustrate the pain that negative self-talk does to you.... when you finish with the negativity about yourself, tear the illustration out and crumple it into the smallest ball that you can.

Once you have it as small as you can get it, you realize that constant negative talk takes away your confidence, your self-esteem and your personal power.

You want to take your words back.... so un-crumple it and smooth out your image. Get it as flat as possible to get rid of the negativity.

You now realize that tiny crumple lines remain... and that's what constant negative self-talk does... it starts to damage your personal power.

Negative self-talk erodes self-esteem and takes away personal power.

We become what we think about ourselves
and what we think of ourselves is the kind of life we live...
so it's important to make adjustments to our inner
negative self-talk.

Suppose your best friend has the same negative beliefs that you have about yourself. What would you say to him/her?

What would s/he say to you if s/he knew you had those negative self- beliefs about yourself?

If you wouldn't say it to your friend... don't think it...or say it about yourself.

Write the four most important positive thoughts that you want to have about yourself.

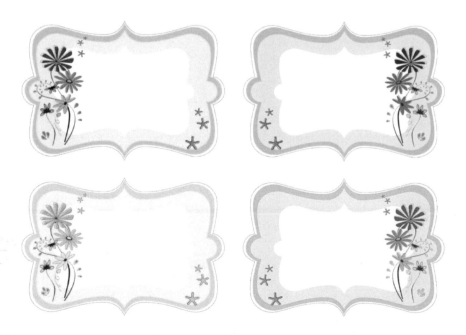

Healthy Relationships

Everyone deserves to be in a safe and healthy relationship not only with friends and classmates, but also in romantic relationships from the very moment a relationship begins.

In unhealthy relationships...
teen & 'tween dating abusers use physical, emotional, digital, sexual or stalking tools to control another person.

Physical abuse —
hitting, punching
slapping, shoving
kicking

Emotional abuse —
threats, name calling,
screaming, yelling,
ridiculing, spreading
rumors, isolation,
intimidation, stalking

Sexual abuse —
unwanted touching
or kissing, forced or
coerced acts

Digital Abuse:
the use of technologies and/or social media networking to intimidate, harass or threaten a partner -such as demanding passwords, checking cell phones, cyberbullying, non-consensual sexting, excessive or threatening texts or stalking on social media

You have the right...

...not to be abused
...to be treated with respect
...to say no
...to express your opinions.
...to spend time with friends and family
...to change your mind
...to fall out of love

The keys to a healthy relationship include communication, trust, and respect.
Describe what your ideal healthy relationship would look like.

The Power and Control Wheel at

http://www.loveisrespect.org/is-this-abuse/power-and-control-wheel/ is a tool that helps explain the different ways an abusive partner can use power and control to manipulate a relationship.

You can click each spoke of the wheel to learn more about the forms of abuse, including examples and red flags.

Warning Signs of Abuse
www.loveisrespect.org

It can be hard to tell when a behavior crosses the line from healthy to unhealthy or even abusive. Use these warning signs of abuse to see if your relationship is going in the wrong direction:

- Checking your cell phone or email without permission
- Constantly putting you down
- Extreme jealousy or insecurity
- Explosive temper
- Isolating you from family or friends
- Making false accusations
- Mood swings
- Physically hurting you in any way
- Possessiveness
- Telling you what to do
- Pressuring or forcing you to do things

So much more information can be found on:

www.loveisrespect.org

If you or a friend is in a relationship that may not be healthy and you need support or information, the website www.loveisrespect.org has highly-trained peer advocates to offer support, information and advocacy to young people.

You or your friend can reach them:
Call 1-866-331-9474
Chat by clicking on the "Chat Online Now" button at the top of the page or
Text: loveis (capitalization does not matter) to 22522

If you feel you or a friend might be in an unhealthy relationship, remember, there is no reason to feel any shame.
This can happen to anyone.
Don't blame yourself — it's not your fault.

You might think that if you just change the way you are – then you will fix the relationship — but no matter what you do, usually the other person won't change.

Also, remember you have options.
You have the right to be in a safe and healthy relationship and the right to end an unhealthy one.

It may not be easy to break up with a controlling partner but http://www.loveisrespect.org can help if you want to talk/text: (loveis to 22522) about it.

Abuse in all forms erodes self-esteem and takes away personal power.

The good news is that this journey of self-exploration is guiding you in discovering new information, thoughts and skills which will improve your confidence, self-esteem and personal power and to better equip you to make healthy relationship choices.

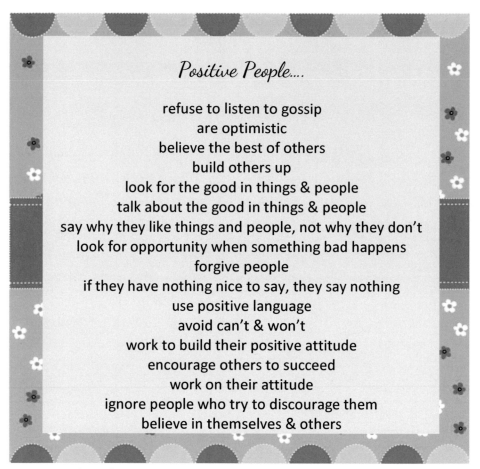

Positive People....

refuse to listen to gossip
are optimistic
believe the best of others
build others up
look for the good in things & people
talk about the good in things & people
say why they like things and people, not why they don't
look for opportunity when something bad happens
forgive people
if they have nothing nice to say, they say nothing
use positive language
avoid can't & won't
work to build their positive attitude
encourage others to succeed
work on their attitude
ignore people who try to discourage them
believe in themselves & others

Identify people you know of all ages, who have some of these
positive characteristics and describe what you admire about them.

Super Special

Is it sometimes easier to point out your own flaws than to point out your good points?

Write down positive characteristics about yourself. Simply note the things that are super special about you. (Examples: smart, kind, a good friend, etc.)

How might being a positive person show you have strong personal power?

 *Emotional Masks*

Does your personality ever change when you're around different individuals or groups?

It's like putting a mask on.

Think about the masks that some people you know wear.
Maybe one wears a mask of being overly responsible to
      cover their pain?
Or maybe one wears a mask of silliness to cover
      self-doubt?
Maybe one wears a mask of troublemaker to cover
       problems at home?
Maybe one wears a mask of a bullying to cover a hurting heart
       because someone has called him/her hurtful names or
       made fun of their weight?

Can you think of other emotional masks someone might wear?

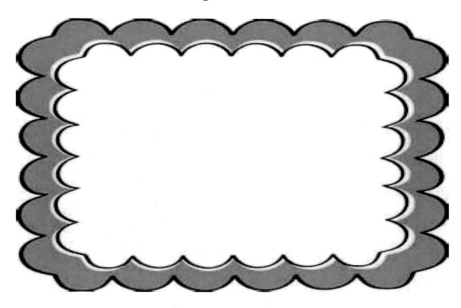

Think about the masks that you might wear in your various life roles.

Do you sometimes try to hide your true self at home to keep from getting in trouble?

Maybe you sometimes wear a mask at school so that you fit in?

What about around boys?
Around girls?
Around teachers?

Self- Harming Masks
Self-harming behaviors may also be masks. Almost any behavior can be used as a mask and some examples include gossiping, lying, cutting, stealing, body image problems, fear, guilt, shame, smoking, alcohol, drug abuse, anger, and the list goes on.

Can you think of other self-harming masks?

How might masks cover up someone's authentic self?

Are there any masks you would like to eliminate so that you can be your true authentic self at all times?

Describe yourself when you are your true authentic self around each.

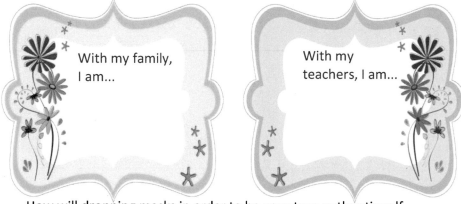

With my family, I am...

With my teachers, I am...

How will dropping masks in order to be your true authentic self increase your self-esteem?

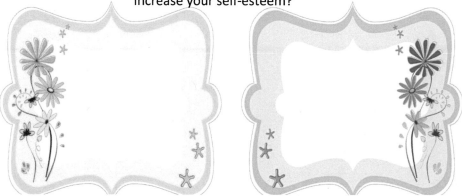

Media and Body Image
Media pressure plays a big role in influencing girls about body image.

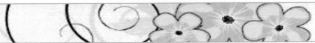

You are surrounded by media images of super-slim teen celebrities, fashion models, beauty and diet commercials and they all work together to try to convince you to buy their products. They also want you to see the images they provide as the norm for happiness.

How can you combat the advertising that tries to manipulate you into believing that your looks determine success and happiness?

Body Image and Real Women and Real Teen Celebrities.

There are many celebrities who are not super-slim and they represent real women and teens.

Some of them include: Adele, Beyonce, Christina Aguilera, Jennifer Hudson, Jennifer Lopez, Jennifer Love Hewitt, Kelly Clarkson, Kim Kardashian, Mariah Carey, Renee Sellweger, Rihanna, Scarlett Johansson, Tyra Banks.

Identify 3 women or teens that you personally admire that are of average size or larger.

Describe their inner qualities (besides beauty) that make them successful. Do they have strong self-esteem?

**Adapted from Mayo Clinic
Healthy body image: Tips for guiding girls**

Help establish healthy eating habits. Exercise and eat a healthy diet for your health, not just to look a certain way.

Counter negative media messages. Think about what you read and watch as well as the products you buy.

Value what you do, rather than what you look like.

Praise your efforts, skills and achievements.

Physical activity. Participating in physical activities — particularly those that don't emphasize a particular weight or body shape — can help promote good self-esteem and a positive body image.

http://www.mayoclinic.com/health/healthy-body-image/MY01225

What are your honest thoughts about how the above tips could affect your self-esteem.

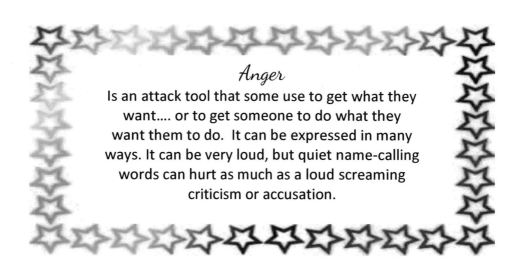

Anger

Is an attack tool that some use to get what they
want…. or to get someone to do what they
want them to do. It can be expressed in many
ways. It can be very loud, but quiet name-calling
words can hurt as much as a loud screaming
criticism or accusation.

Anger drama takes a lot of energy. Have you ever seen the drama of
someone throwing a 'fit' to get what they wanted? What might it look
and sound like?

Have you witnessed someone carrying on to make a parent feel guilty
so they will do what they want them to do? What might it look and
sound like?

Have you ever seen a child hit or kick someone to get what they
want? What might it look and sound like?

words have power

In The Anger Habit Workbook, Carl Semmelroth Ph.D. writes that anger attacks are problem solving tools and that anger impairs the IQ.

The attacks lead to a life of accumulating power in order to control others.

His Workbook leads to solving problems such as reminding yourself that being in an attack mode means that you are not as smart in that moment, and that you're going to take a 15 minute time out... for your intelligence to return.

The problem that led to your attack mode will still be there in 15 minutes but a more intelligent you will there to solve the problem.

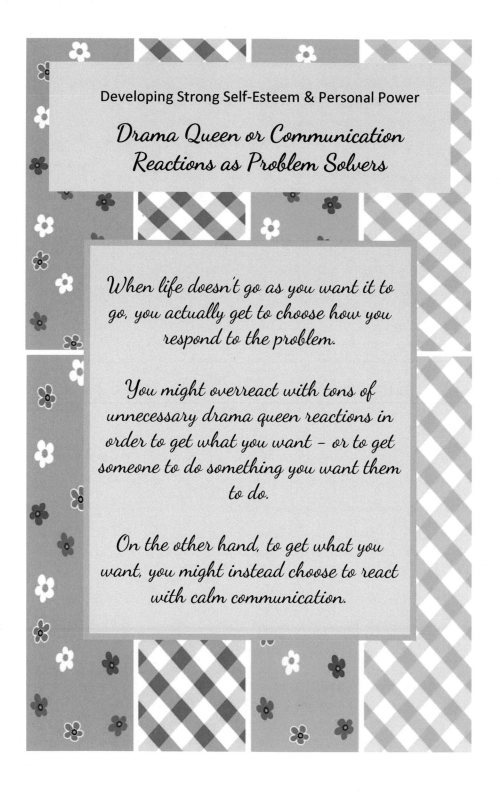

Developing Strong Self-Esteem & Personal Power

Drama Queen or Communication Reactions as Problem Solvers

When life doesn't go as you want it to go, you actually get to choose how you respond to the problem.

You might overreact with tons of unnecessary drama queen reactions in order to get what you want – or to get someone to do something you want them to do.

On the other hand, to get what you want, you might instead choose to react with calm communication.

Drama Queen Anger Reaction:

Even though you may not be a drama queen problem solver....descrIbe what a drama-queen reaction might look and sound like as you try to solve your problem of getting your mom to do something you want her to do after she has said 'no'.

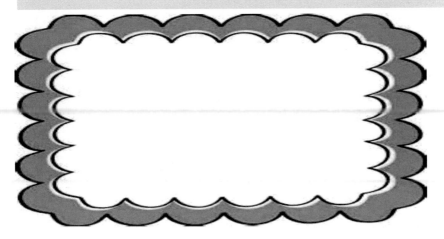

Drama-Free Communication Reaction:

Even though you may not be a communication problem solver, describe what your reaction might look and sound like as you try to get your mom to do something you want her to do after she has said 'no'...
by calmly communicating.

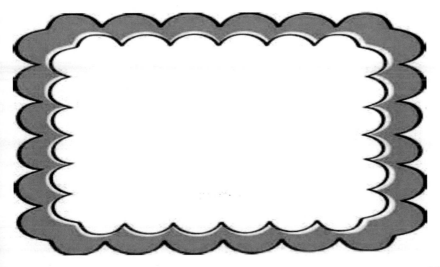

Pick one time when you totally freaked out about something and explain how you responded to the incidence.

How might have you reacted differently?

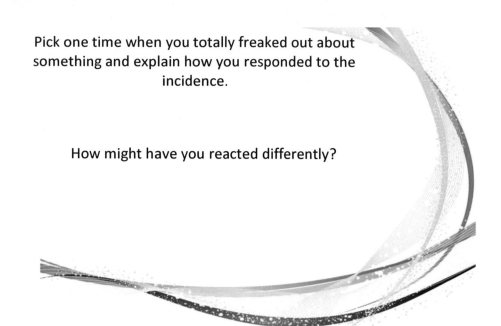

Think of someone you know that is a drama queen problem solver... have you ever noticed if she uses it only with certain people?

Are there people in her life that she never uses drama-queen reactions with?

What might the differences in those people be?

Maybe some expect the drama-queen reaction?

Would some act as though they can't do anything about the way she reacts?

Which type of problem solving do you believe actually has a better chance of getting what you want while earning respect from others?

How does that type of problem solving grow your self-esteem and personal power?

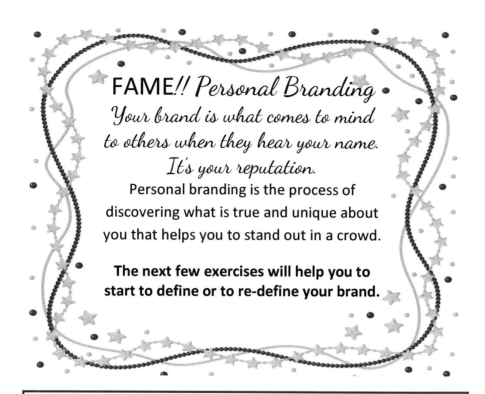

FAME!! Personal Branding

Your brand is what comes to mind to others when they hear your name.
It's your reputation.

Personal branding is the process of discovering what is true and unique about you that helps you to stand out in a crowd.

The next few exercises will help you to start to define or to re-define your brand.

Branding is not about changing who you are, but it is about becoming more of who you are by discovering... or re-discovering your true authentic self.

It's important that you build your own brand before someone else does.

Think about how often kids get teased by name-calling and then those words become the kid's brand. Words like loser and fat, do not reflect anyone's true inner self.

How has someone branded you with qualities that did not reflect your true self?

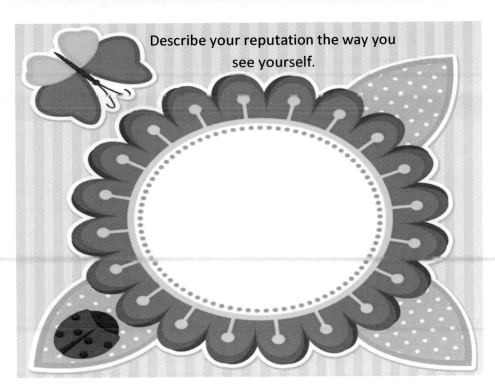

Describe your reputation the way you see yourself.

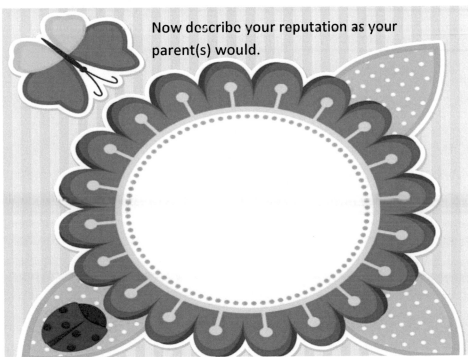

Now describe your reputation as your parent(s) would.

Your personal brand is built on a foundation of your values.

Values That Help You Live Your Life

___ APPRECIATION	___ FAMILY	___ FRIENDSHIP
___ HEALTH	___ INTEGRITY	___ LOVE
___ POLITE	___ RESPONSIBLE	___ TOLERANCE
___ UNITY	___ COMPASSION	___ FAIRNESS
___ FORGIVENESS	___ GENEROSITY	___ HONESTY
___ KINDNESS	___ LOYALTY	___ RELIABLE
___ SELF-DISCIPLINE	___ TRUSTWORTHY	___ WISDOM
___ COOPERATION	___ FAITH	___ FREEDOM
___ HARMONY	___ HUMOR	___ HELPING
___ RESPECT	___ SHARING	___ TRUTH
___ FAITHFULNESS	___FORWARD LOOKING	___ COMMUNITY
___ CARING	___ CALM	___DETERMINED
___ DECENT	___ EMPOWERED	___ PEACEFUL
___ PATIENT	___ PERSISTENT	___ POSITIVE
___SINCERITY	___POWERFUL	___RISK TAKING
___RESPECT	___RESOURCEFUL	___ SELF-ESTEEM

Check 10 values that apply to you at this time in your life but don't be limited by the list. Add other values that feel right for you.

Clarifying Your Core Values
Of the values listed, did you find some that instantly jolted you and you immediately circled them?

Of your ten, narrow them down to your top three values.

1. _____
2. _____
3. _____

Strengths are internal and along with your core values, they help to identify your brand. Describe your strengths.

Life Passions

Now, let's move to your life passions that are your interests and the things you love to do.

They are more of an outer symbol that makes it easier for others to see who you are because your passions show your personality.
List your passions that you love and help to make you.... you.

Talents and Skills

Another important part of your brand that helps set you apart
includes your talents and your skills. What are you really good at?
What skills make you special or unique? Don't forget to include
skills and talents you use in school or in your other life roles.

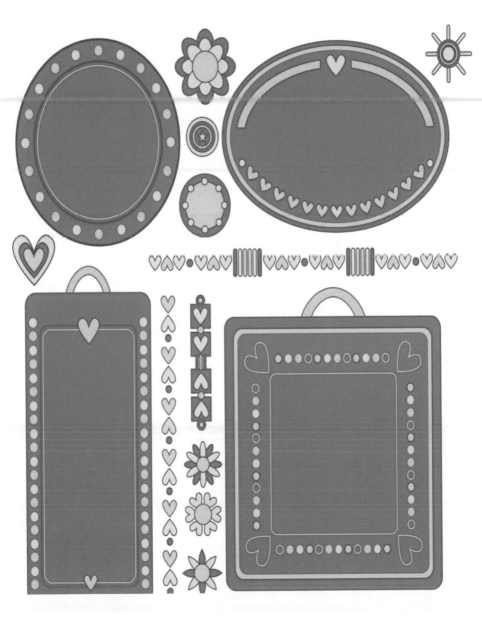

Write Your Brand Description

Review your branding worksheets and use your strongest characteristics, values, passions and talents to describe the confident 'you' that you want to project to others. Describe yourself as you would like others to describe you.

Examples:

- I am a passionate and creative student who brings my leadership skills to our school in order to create a positive environment in our classroom and throughout the whole school so that every student feels that they have a place to belong.

- I use my enthusiasm and my love of animals to help other kids and adults in our community develop an awareness about ways we all can do something to help abused animals in our area.

My Brand... My Authentic Self

Project Your Brand

With your personality, attitudes, body language and style, describe how will you project your brand to the world through your thoughts, your words, your behaviors and your actions?

Developing stronger confidence, self-esteem and personal power is a life-long learning process.

With these first steps on your journey - how might you now use your personal power in each area from page 5?

Being assertive so that your ideas are heard and you can respectfully challenge the ideas of others.

Expressing ideas and reasons to convince someone of your point of view.

Making compromises and concessions to reach outcomes that satisfy your integrity.

Building respectful relationships.

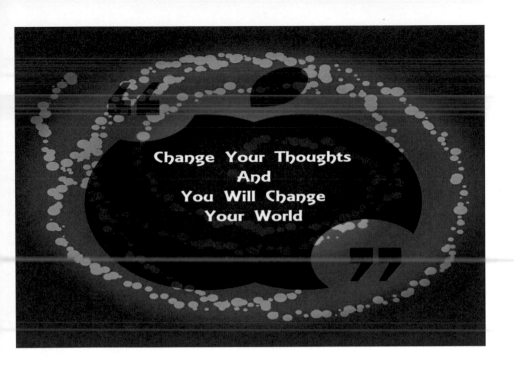

"Change Your Thoughts
And
You Will Change
Your World"

This inner journey to positive personal power started with a saying..."we become what we think about" and another saying of "knowledge is power".

Your journey of self-discovery continued on with activities to help you learn and to better understand the importance of changing negative inner thinking into positive thinking that leads to positive personal power.

In life... we never stop learning and this workbook serves as an educational foundation for you to continue on your lifetime journey of empowerment.

The final exercise provides an opportunity to identify two goals to work on as it relates to continuing to build your confidence, self-esteem and personal power... as you continue on your everyday life journey.

A goal is something that you want to be, to have or to do.
Ensure your goal is specific. (To get.... To be...etc.)
Express your goal positively.

Your first goal:

_____

_____

What will achieving your goal mean to you? What would it look
...feel...sound like?

What specific steps would you commit to and work hard for, in order to
achieve your goal?

What roadblocks/fears have prevented you from reaching this goal in the
past?

What specific actions can you take to work around each roadblock?

Describe your skills or other resources that are available to you that would
help you to achieve your goal.

What other resources might you need?

Describe steps that you can take to keep yourself on track in reaching this
goal.

A goal is something that you want to be, to have or to do.
Ensure your goal is specific. (To get.... To be...etc.)
Express your goal positively.

Your second goal:

_____

_____

What will achieving your goal mean to you? What would it look
feel, sound like?

What specific steps would you commit to and work hard for, in order to achieve your goal?

What roadblocks/fears have prevented you from reaching this goal in the past?

What specific actions can you take to work around each roadblock?

Describe your skills or other resources that are available to you that would help you to achieve your goal.

What other resources might you need?

Describe steps that you can take to keep yourself on track in reaching this goal.

SOOOO You!!

You have finished this leg of your life-journey in order to increase your confidence, self-esteem and personal power.

You are SOOOOO you and you will continue to journey and to live your life from your heart.

let's go for a ride

Personal Power Workbooks and Life Coaching Journals by Martie Morris Lee

The youth and adult workbooks and journals are for home use and also for use in groups, organizations and agencies.

Workbooks

Your Journey to Personal Power Workbook (Teen Girls)
Personal Power... for Guys (Teens)
Cap'n Jack's Journey to Personal Power Workbook (2nd to 6th)
Bullying – The Power of One Workbook (1st to 3rd)
Hands & Words Are Not for Hurting - Good Hands Club Workbook.
(Pre-School to 1st Grade)
Positively Empowered! (Women)

Life Coaching Journals
My Dance... My Journey Journal for Women (Life Coaching)
Life Coaching Journal for Teen Girls
Life Coaching Journal for 'Tween Girls
Life Coaching Journal for Teen Guys
Life Coaching Journal for Men

Made in the USA
Middletown, DE
12 March 2017